Origins

Tiger's Discovery

Michaela Morgan ✷ Jonatronix

OXFORD
UNIVERSITY PRESS

In this story ...

Tiger

Miss Jones
(Tiger's teacher)

Mrs Mills
(the head teacher)

Tiger was late for school. As he passed the staffroom he heard voices.

"Where do you think you lost it?" said Mrs Mills.

"I don't know," said Miss Jones. She sounded very upset.

Staffroom

Tiger wondered what Miss Jones had lost.
He looked into the staffroom.

"What does it look like?" asked Mrs Mills.

Miss Jones held out her hand. Something sparkled.

"What a shame!" said Mrs Mills.

"I'll have to look for my earring later," said Miss Jones.

The bell went for class. Tiger hid. Mrs Mills and Miss Jones came out of the staffroom and shut the door.

Tiger didn't like to see Miss Jones upset. He had an idea. He turned the dial on his watch and ...

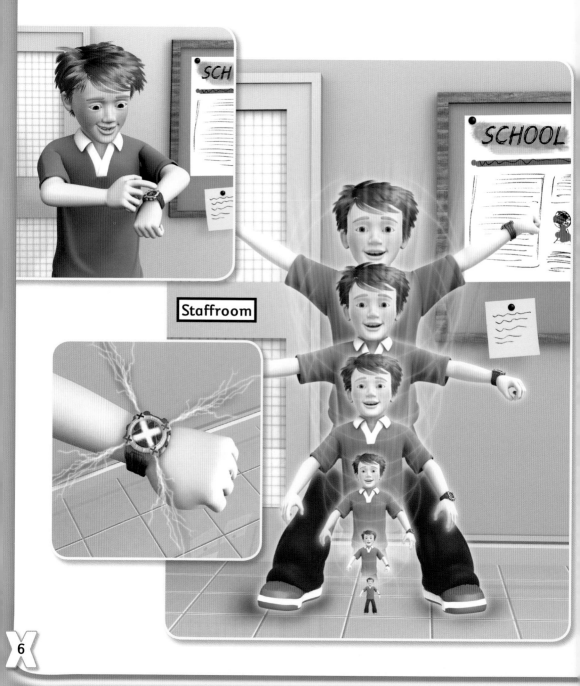

How Children Learn

Plays for Assemblies

Fairy Tales

A micro-sized Tiger crawled under the door. He had never been in the staffroom before. It was a bit scary. He looked all around hoping to see the sparkly earring.

Just then, the door opened. Mrs Mills was back!
"Oh, no!" cried Tiger.
He ran and hid behind the bin.

"What a mess!" Mrs Mills said.
"No wonder Miss Jones can't find her earring."
Mrs Mills picked up some rubbish and walked towards the bin. Tiger had to move … fast!

Tiger ran across to the table. He looked up. Something sparkled! It was on top of a pile of papers.

"There it is!" he said.

How Children Learn

Eco Gardens for Schools

Plays for Assemblies

Fairy Tales

Mrs Mills had her back turned.
Tiger began to climb.
It was hard work.
Finally he got
to the top …
and what
sparkly thing
did he find?

Lessons

It was a drawing pin.

"Oh, no!" Tiger groaned.

Then the pile of paper tipped. Tiger started to slip.

"Help!" cried Tiger.

He tipped and slipped and tumbled down.

splosh!

SPLOSH!
Tiger landed in a mug of cold tea. It was a good job he could swim.
"How am I going to get out of here?" he said.

He did not have to wait long. Mrs Mills came over. "What a mess!" she said. She picked up the mug. "Oh, no!" said Tiger. He held his breath and ducked down in the cold tea.

How Children Learn

Eco Gardens for Schools

Plays for Assemblies

Fairy Tales

Mrs Mills tipped the cold tea into the sink. *SPLASH!*

Tiger swirled round and round. He was pulled towards the plughole …

splash!

"Help!" cried Tiger. He grabbed hold of the plug and hung on tight. The tea gurgled down the plughole.

When it was gone, Tiger climbed down in to the sink.

Help!

The sink was a bit grubby. There was a mug and some spoons and … what was that? Something sparkled!

It was the earring!

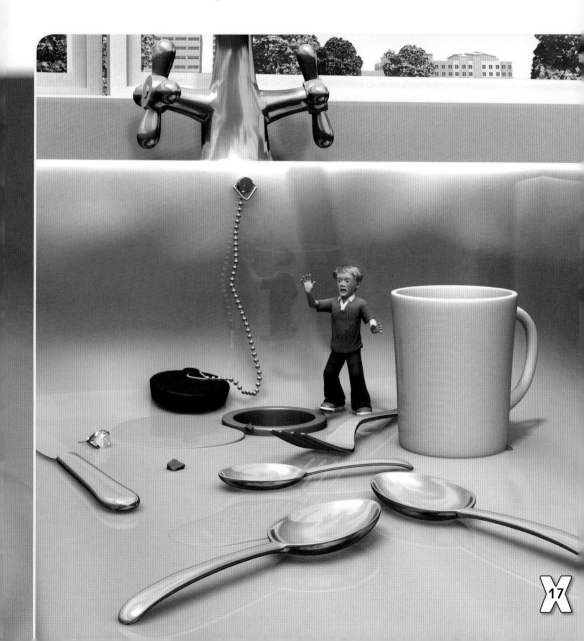

Tiger picked up the earring. He climbed up the plug chain and out of the sink. Then he climbed down a hand towel. He ran across the staffroom and crawled under the door.

Back in the corridor, Tiger put down the earring. He turned the dial on his watch and …

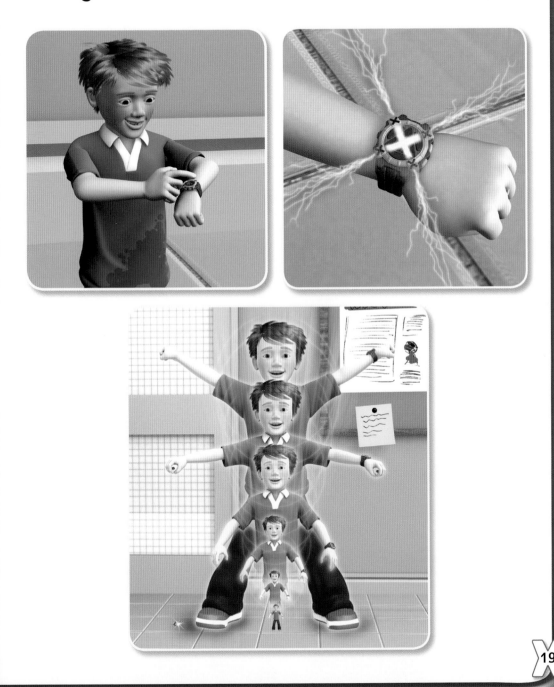

Tiger picked up the earring. He hurried along to his classroom.

"Tiger!" said Miss Jones, crossly. "Why are you so late? And why are you all dirty and wet?"

"Sorry, Miss Jones," said Tiger. "I fell in a puddle."

Tiger held out his hand.

"But I found this," he said. "Has anyone lost it?"

"My earring!" said Miss Jones. She sounded very happy. "Oh, thank you, Tiger!"

3 J

Retell the story ...

4

5

6

Find out more ...

For more amazing discoveries read:
The Silver Box

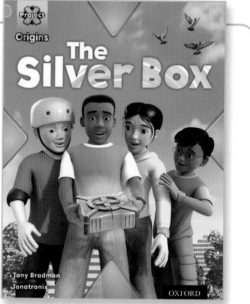

and *Finding Things!*